D1497384

carte blanche
greetings ltd ®

© 2009 Carte Blanche Greetings Ltd ®

www.carteblanchegreetings.com

First edition for the United States published in 2010 by Barron's Educational Series, Inc.

First published in the U.K. by HarperCollins Children's Books in 2009 under the title: *Me to You—Best Dad.*

The Me to You oval, Tatty Teddy signature, and bear logo are all registered trademarks of Carte Blanche Greetings Ltd.
© Carte Blanche Greetings Ltd ® P.O. Box 500, Chichester, PO20 2XZ, U.K.

All inquiries should be addressed to:
Barron's Educational Series, Inc.
250 Wireless Boulevard
Hauppauge, NY 11788
www.barronseduc.com

ISBN-13: 978-0-7641-6293-0
ISBN-10: 0-7641-6293-4

Printed in China
9 8 7 6 5 4 3 2 1

Best Dad

BARRON'S

A dad is the best friend
you'll ever find.

Dads HAVE All
tHE facts!

Through good times
and bad, dads are
always there.

Dads help us to celebrate
our successes.

Dads always help to
make things right.

If something is broken,
dad can always fix it.

Dads are always there
to sort things out.

When people think of safety and warmth, they think of dad.

Dads always
lend a helping hand.

Dads are always
ready to play!

Dads are special,
and you are the most
special dad of all!

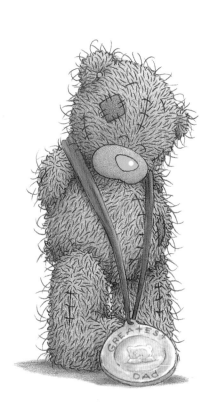

You're my number one, dad!